Eagles

Diane Swanson

Gareth Stevens Publishing
A WORLD ALMANAC EDUCATION GROUP COMPANY

Please visit our web site at: www.garethstevens.com
For a free color catalog describing Gareth Stevens Publishing's list of high-quality books and multimedia programs, call 1-800-542-2595 (USA) or 1-800-387-3178 (Canada). Gareth Stevens Publishing's fax: (414) 332-3567.

The publishers acknowledge the support of the Canada Council for the Arts and the Cultural Services Branch of the Government of British Columbia in making this publication possible.

Library of Congress Cataloging-in-Publication Data

Swanson, Diane, 1944-
   [Welcome to the world of eagles]
   Eagles / by Diane Swanson. — North American ed.
     p. cm. — (Welcome to the world of animals)
   Includes index.
   Summary: Describes the physical characteristics, behavior, habitat, and life cycle of bald and golden eagles.
   ISBN 0-8368-3561-1 (lib. bdg.)
   1. Eagles—Juvenile literature. [1. Eagles.] I. Title.
   QL696.F32S98   2003
   598.9'42—dc21   2002030277

This edition first published in 2003 by
Gareth Stevens Publishing
A World Almanac Education Group Company
330 West Olive Street, Suite 100
Milwaukee, WI 53212 USA

This U.S. edition © 2003 by Gareth Stevens, Inc. Original edition © 1998 by Diane Swanson. First published in 1998 by Whitecap Books, Vancouver. Additional end matter © 2003 by Gareth Stevens, Inc.

Series editor: Lauren Fox
Design: Katherine A. Goedheer
Cover design: Renee M. Bach

Cover photograph: Thomas Kitchin/Firstlight
Photo credits: Thomas Kitchin/First Light 4, 22; Tim Christie 6; Wayne Lynch 8, 26, 28; Lynn M. Stone 10, 12, 14, 18, 20, 24, 30; S. Osolinski/First Light 16

Printed in the United States of America

1 2 3 4 5 6 7 8 9 07 06 05 04 03

# Contents

World of Difference

Look up high to see eagles in the sky. With strong wings beating deeply, they take off into the wind. They rise higher and higher, then hold their wings steady and g-l-i-d-e.

Eagles catch rides on big bubbles of warm, rising air. The birds spiral up and up until they disappear from sight. Then they swoop down and ride back up again.

The eagle is one of the biggest birds on Earth. With wings outstretched, an eagle can easily span the length of your bed. But it usually weighs no more than a small dog—about 13 pounds (6 kilograms).

Around the world, there are about sixty different kinds of eagles. In North

A master of flight, the bald eagle seems to rule the sky.

A black tip marks the thick beak of the golden eagle.

America, there are just two kinds: golden eagles and bald eagles. Both were named for the color of feathers on their necks and heads. "White" is one meaning of the word "bald."

Worldwide, golden eagles belong to a group known as booted eagles. Unlike other kinds, their legs and feet are covered with feathers. Bald eagles belong to a group of fishing eagles. The bottoms of their feet are rough, making it easier to hold onto slippery fish.

All eagles feed on meat. Both golden and bald eagles have strong feet that are as large as human hands. They have hooked claws — called talons — for nabbing and killing prey. Eagles also have curved, pointed beaks for tearing flesh.

POWER POLE EAGLES

Eagles sometimes perch on poles instead of trees. Many of these poles are strung with wires that carry electricity. If an eagle's wings touch two of these wires at once: ZAP! Electricity flows through its body, usually killing the bird — especially if its wings are wet.

People are working to make power poles safer. Some put up landing bars so eagles can perch above the wires. Some set up barriers so that eagles can't perch between the wires.

7

Where in the World

Eagles live where eagles eat. Bald eagles usually live close to water because fish is their main food. They hunt along oceans, lakes, and rivers.

Golden eagles eat a variety of prey, so they can hunt almost anywhere: in mountains, open forests, grasslands, and deserts. They seem to prefer hilly areas, where they can easily grab rides on the rising air.

Both kinds of eagles have territories — areas where they live and hunt. They guard their territories from other eagles, even attacking invaders if they must.

High places, like a branch on this tall tree in Florida, make good lookouts for eagles.

9

Wintry weather doesn't bother bald eagles as long as the rivers still flow with fish.

When eagles rest or nest, they head for tree branches or ledges on rocky cliffs. Some even perch on poles. But if there are no trees, cliffs, or poles around, they may just settle on the ground.

In spring and fall, many eagles head for new places to feed. Some fly south for the winter, where it is easier to find food.

But in Florida, where the weather is warm year-round, adult bald eagles usually stay put.

Except for Antarctica, every continent is home to eagles of one kind or another. In the past, there were more eagles than there are now, and they lived in more places. Today, most bald eagles in North America live along the northwest coast. Golden eagles live across most of Canada, in the western United States, and in parts of Mexico, Europe, Asia, and Africa.

GOLDEN JOURNEY

In 1992, a bird-watcher in Canada discovered the world's longest flight path for golden eagles. Each fall, up to ten thousand golden eagles fly south along the Rocky Mountains as far as Mexico. Then in spring, they head north as far as the Arctic.

Traveling up to 435 miles (700 kilometers) a day, the eagles save energy by spiraling on air bubbles above the mountain peaks, then gliding down. They sometimes glide a long way before they spiral up again.

World of the Hunter

Eagles make great hunters. From the sky, their sharp eyes can spot fish in the water and mice on the ground. Eagles also have all the tools they need to catch their prey.

With wings folded back, the eagle dives at its target. Just before striking, its feet swing forward. Toes with razor-sharp talons nab the prey. One blow from the talon on the back toe is usually enough to kill.

The eagle often flies to a perch to eat its catch — unless the food is too heavy to carry. Using its sharp beak, the eagle may strip off the fur or feathers of its prey before ripping it apart.

Swoop. Snatch. This bald eagle has a fish for dinner.

13

Although the beak gets worn down by plenty of hard use, it never wears out. Like the eagle's talons, it keeps growing as long as the eagle lives — up to twenty-five years.

Bald eagles often wade into shallow water to grab dead fish. They also swoop down and snatch live fish, sometimes plunging into the water for prey.

A young bald eagle — feathered in colors different from an adult's — is a keen fisher.

If the eagles get too wet to fly, they swim back to shore, paddling with their wings. Besides fish, bald eagles also eat some of the same foods that golden eagles eat: rabbits, rats, snakes, turtles — even garbage. They sometimes also attack young wolves, deer, and sheep.

Eagles mostly hunt alone, but at times they work in pairs. One might scare prey out of hiding, while the other attacks it. Or the eagles might just steal dinner from other birds, including other eagles.

DANGER: FALLING FOOD!

A story from ancient Greece told of a poet who was warned: "Be careful! A house may fall and kill you." All day, the poet stayed away from buildings.

A flying eagle mistook the poet's bald head for a large stone and dropped a turtle on it. Sure enough, the blow from the turtle's "house" — its hard shell — killed the poet. Eagles often drop animals such as turtles and clams to crack open their shells. Then they can eat the soft insides.

World of Words

Eagle eggs chirp. Then eagle mothers chirp back. They know the eaglets are almost ready to break out of their eggs. Soon after the eaglets hatch, their chirps turn to squawks as they holler for food.

Like other animals, eagles talk to each other by making different calls and by moving their bodies in different ways. Golden eagles, which spend most of their time alone, make calls less often than bald eagles. But both kinds call out as they court their mates, spot other eagles in their territories, and guard their food.

To say, "Don't eat my lunch," eagles stare, fluff out their feathers, and scream.

Bald eagles use their hearing more when talking than when hunting.

17

The golden eagle is making a threat: "Stay away from my prey."

Their message is especially clear if they are standing on top of their food at the time.

When eagles soar through the sky, they seldom talk at all. But as they approach their nests, bald eagles make squeaky noises, over and over again. They seem to be announcing, "Here I come." Golden eagles also make yelping noises near their nests, mainly when they are bringing home food.

If an eagle has been tending its eggs for quite a while, it may cry to its mate to say, "Let's trade places." It may also dive at its mate to be sure the mate understands.

But it's easiest for eagles to say, "I'm hot." Like a dog, the eagle just lets its mouth hang open. Then it dangles its tongue and pants.

GATHERING, BLATHERING

"Keeree-ree-ik-ik-ik-ik," scream the eagles in the trees. "Keeree-ree-ik-ik-ik-ik," scream the eagles on the ground. All this noise goes on between bites of dinner. The calls grow loudest when eagles get close to each other.

Each fall, thousands of bald eagles gather and squawk loudly along a few rivers that flow thick with salmon. After the fish deposit and fertilize their eggs, they die — and become meals for the hungry eagles.

World of Mates

Eagles take their mates sky dancing. Together, a couple soars, swoops, glides, and dives through the air. One eagle may follow the other, or one may swoop while the other soars. At times, the lower bird flips over so its talons can reach those of the bird above it. The two may even grip each other's toes and cartwheel down together — almost tumbling to the ground.

For both golden and bald eagles, the bond between mates usually lasts a lifetime. Each year, they return to the same place — often to the same nest — to raise their families.

Eagle mates share a quiet moment as they perch in a tree.

Both kinds of eagles prefer nests in tall trees or on ledges along steep cliffs, which make the best lookouts. Bald eagles also like nests close to water, where they hunt.

The pair often works together to build a big nest of branches and sticks. If the eagles reuse a nest, they enlarge it first and line it again with

Home sweet home for a bald eagle is a gigantic nest, built high in a tree.

fresh grass, moss, and pine needles. Bald eagles sometimes add seaweed to the lining. Then the nest is ready to cradle their eggs. The female usually lays two eggs in the spring. Both mates warm them and keep them safe.

Eagles sometimes have guests in or near their nests. Small birds, such as house sparrows, sometimes make homes on the outside of a nest while eagles are inside. After the eagles move out, the nest may become home to other guests: owls, squirrels, or raccoons.

JUMBO NESTS

If you tried to build an eagle nest, you would soon discover how huge it is. At one nursery school, fourteen children gathered sticks to make a bald eagle nest — just for fun. Together, they formed a line that reached only halfway around the nest.

After a storm knocked down one bald eagle's nest, people rebuilt it. They wove sticks into a wire frame and lined it with grass. The nest was three times deeper than a bathtub, and it weighed 200 pounds (90 kilograms).

New World

Breaking out of an egg takes hours of work. Eaglets are ready to eat soon after they hatch. The mother feeds her young tiny bits of flesh, torn from prey that the father catches.

At first, the mother stays close to her eaglets, keeping them safe under her wings. She makes sure they're not too cold and not too hot. She protects them from other animals, such as owls. But before very long, she leaves them alone for a while as she helps her mate hunt.

When the eaglets are a few weeks old, the mother eagle brings food to the nest

Mealtime comes often for the bald eaglets in this ground nest in Alaska.

and then starts to eat it herself. The hungry eaglets scream and squawk. Then they drape their wings over the food and tear off small pieces. They soon learn to feed themselves.

As their wings get stronger, the eaglets flap them a lot. Sometimes they flap so much that the eaglets lift themselves up off their feet. Day by day, the little birds rise higher above the nest.

A golden eaglet changes its coat from white, fuzzy down to dark feathers.

Soon the eaglets are flying, and they are ready to learn how to hunt. They watch their parents grab a snake, a fish, or other animal. Then they try to do the same.

At first, the eaglets miss their prey, but their hunting skills gradually improve. They even learn to steal food from crows and other eagles, just as their parents do.

By fall, the eaglets are ready to find their own food and, years later, their own mates. The young eagles are ready to be part of a much bigger world.

FLYING LESSONS

Teaching an eaglet to fly takes time. A parent eagle may circle its nest, clutching a fish. That makes the eaglet in the nest squawk and flap its wings. The parent keeps circling and flying off until the eaglet chases the fish.

The eaglet flies as far as it can before landing. As it rests, the parent eagle feeds it the fish. Then both birds return to the nest. Each day, the parent draws the eaglet farther away from the nest until it learns to fly well.

Fun World

Young eagles are eager for fun. They start playing when they are only four or five weeks old. The nest becomes the eaglets' playpen.

At first, the eaglets just crawl around, exploring the nest. As they grow bigger and stronger, they start hopping about. And when they're able to flap their wings hard, the eaglets can rise above the nest. Up and down they go — like children jumping on a trampoline.

Eaglets have plenty of "toys": feathers, twigs, leaves, bones, fish heads, scraps of fur, and bits of leftover food. Playing alone,

A feather? A twig? Which toys will these golden eaglets play with next?

an eaglet tosses its toys around with its beak. It heaves them into the air, then grabs them when they land in the nest. It attacks them as if they were prey. Sometimes the eaglet uses its beak to catch and crush the toys. Other times, it uses its talons and toes to pounce on the toys or snatch them.

"That was fun," this bald eagle seems to say after pouncing on some white feathers.

If there are two eaglets in a family, they play together. When one flings a toy, they both try to grab it. If they snatch the toy at the same time, the game may change to tug-of-war. All their romping and stomping usually flattens out the nest.

Spending so much time at play gives the eaglets plenty of exercise. It helps them get ready to fly, and it gives them practice hunting. All that fun helps make life as a full-grown eagle a little easier.

EAGLE WONDERS

Eagles are amazing! Here are some of the reasons why:

- **Extra, see-through eyelids protect an eagle's eyes from dust, rain, and bright light.**

- **Eagles can kill prey four times heavier than they are.**

- **One thirty-six-year-old bald eagle nest in the United States weighed as much as a minivan.**

- **When they build nests, eagles sometimes use rabbit bones as twigs.**

Glossary

bond — something that ties or holds two or more things together.

continent — one of the seven major land masses of the world. North America is one of the continents.

court — (v) to try to attract a mate by doing something that pleases or interests the other animal.

down — the soft feathers covering a bird's body.

fertilize — to make an egg able to grow and develop.

keen — sharp and well developed, as in senses that work quickly and accurately.

mates — (n) pairs of male and female animals that produce young.

perch — (v) to sit or rest on something, such as a branch.

prey — animals hunted by other animals for food.

stomping — stamping your foot or feet against the ground or another surface.

Index